9978

D1396532

Brighter Tomorrows

Program Consultants

Stephanie Abraham Hirsh, Ph.D.
Associate Director
National Staff Development Council
Dallas, Texas

Louise Matteoni, Ph.D.
Professor of Education
Brooklyn College
City University of New York

Karen Tindel Wiggins
Social Studies Consultant
Richardson Independent School District
Richardson, Texas

Renee Levitt
Educational Consultant
Scarsdale, New York

 **Steck-Vaughn
Company**

A Subsidiary of National Education Corporation

MOMENTS IN AMERICAN HISTORY

Brighter Tomorrows

BY
Melissa Stone

Steck-Vaughn Literature Library
Moments in American History

RISKING IT ALL
REBELLION'S SONG
CREATIVE DAYS
RACING TO THE WEST
YOU DON'T OWN ME!
CLOUDS OF WAR
A CRY FOR ACTION
LARGER THAN LIFE
FLYING HIGH
BRIGHTER TOMORROWS

Illustrations: Tom Leonard: cover art, pp. 8-9, 10, 12, 15, 17, 19; Brian Pinkney: pp. 20-21, 23, 25, 26, 29, 31; Steve Cieslawski: pp. 32-33, 35, 37, 38, 41, 43; Al Fiorentino: pp. 44-45, 46, 48, 50, 53, 55; Lyle Miller: pp. 56-57, 59, 60, 62-63, 64, 67; Rae Ecklund: pp. 68-69, 71, 73, 74-75, 77, 79.

Project Editor: Anne Souby

Design: Kirchoff/Wohlberg, Inc.

ISBN 0-8114-4084-2

1 2 3 4 5 6 7 8 9 0 UN 92 91 90 89 88

CONTENTS

1950

◄ **JONAS SALK**
After years of polio research, he put his life on the line for the final test.
(1948-1955)

ROSA PARKS ►
She was tired and her feet hurt. And she started a movement that changed history.
(1955-1956)

◄ **BUDDY HOLLY**
Despite a very brief career, this rock star's influence is still felt today.
(1941-1959)

1970

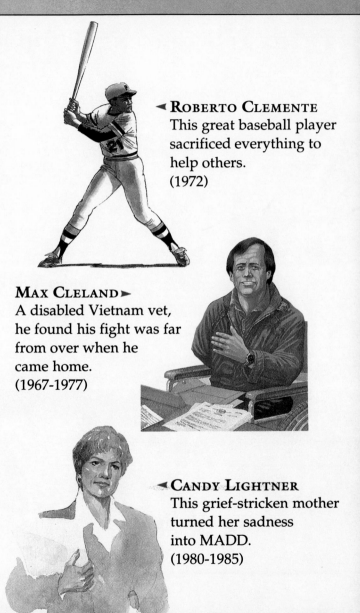

ROBERTO CLEMENTE
This great baseball player sacrificed everything to help others.
(1972)

MAX CLELAND
A disabled Vietnam vet, he found his fight was far from over when he came home.
(1967-1977)

CANDY LIGHTNER
This grief-stricken mother turned her sadness into MADD.
(1980-1985)

JONAS SALK
THE FIGHT AGAINST POLIO

Polio — a horrible raging epidemic! It often strikes young children, crippling them. They can't even breathe without a huge machine, an iron lung! I am a research scientist. My life's work is to conquer diseases. Now I must find a way to prevent polio! If research could only go faster!

W E all know that polio is an infectious disease that attacks the central nervous system. It kills thousands of people each year and leaves many more crippled for life," announced Basil O'Connor to the reporters who crowded around him one sunny day in 1948. "In the ten years I have been head of the National Foundation for Infantile Paralysis, no significant progress has been made toward stopping polio. People are still suffering and dying. Children are still having to live their lives in iron lungs."

"But what can be done about it?" called out one reporter.

"I'm declaring an all-out war against the disease. I believe that if we pour our resources into scientific research, we can find a way to wipe out polio forever."

Wipe out polio? It seemed too fantastic to be possible. When the reporters wrote their columns the next day, many dismissed O'Connor's words as idle talk. But Dr. Jonas Salk, head of the Virus Research Laboratory at the University of Pittsburgh, read and reread O'Connor's speech in the newspaper.

"Yes," thought Dr. Salk with a nod of his head. "Yes, I believe O'Connor is right. If enough researchers attack the problem, surely we can find a way to stop this disease."

Jonas Salk had great faith in the power of research. He liked the clear, logical patterns it followed. He didn't mind conducting the slow, sometimes repetitious experiments required. He knew that a good research scientist needed a calm nature and plenty of patience. Dr. Salk had both.

He decided to accept the challenge. He hurried to contact Basil O'Connor. "I want to join your crusade against polio," he said.

Dr. Salk received funding from the National Foundation for Infantile Paralysis. He used the money to begin an ambitious study of polio.

"We know that viruses cause polio," he told his staff. "But how many different kinds of polio viruses are there? And what are their characteristics? We have much to find out."

For three long years, Salk and his colleagues at other universities experimented. They tested one virus after another. At last, in 1951, they finished the first part of the research.

"We have determined that there are three distinct polio viruses," Salk announced that year. "To protect people against polio, we must protect them from all three viruses."

"The first step is completed," said Salk. "We

know what we're up against. Now we need to concentrate on making a vaccine."

A vaccine is a small amount of a disease virus that can be injected into a person's body. The individual's system then responds by making antibodies to destroy the virus. If the person is ever exposed to the disease again, antibodies will destroy the virus. And the person will be safe from the disease.

S ALK'S sense of urgency increased in 1952 when a huge wave of polio swept the United States. Thousands of people died. Many others were crippled for life.

"We're going to begin work on a *dead*-virus vaccine," Salk announced to his assistants.

"We're going to kill the polio virus before injecting it into test animals?" asked one worker.

"Exactly."

"But, Dr. Salk, all the research states that *live* viruses must be used in vaccines," one assistant objected. "A person's system won't respond properly to dead viruses. The right kind of antibodies won't be produced in the blood."

"I know that's the current belief," Salk replied. "But when I was working on a flu vaccine, I had promising results using the dead virus. I'm convinced it's worth a try."

Salk was one of a handful of researchers who believed a dead-virus vaccine might be effective. Many scientists had built their careers on the opposing view. Salk was challenging long-held scientific beliefs when he publicized his work with dead viruses. Many scientists took offense at his experiments. Some even condemned his research efforts.

"Salk's just wasting time. Time and valuable research money," declared one scientist. "He doesn't have a chance in a million for success."

But Salk knew that research was never wasted. He said, "No well-designed experiment ever fails. We must keep an open mind and, based on whatever findings are made, plan for the next step ahead."

SALK spent the next several weeks working out a way to kill the polio viruses. Then he injected them into test animals. Progress came quickly. Test animals injected with the vaccine did not develop polio. Instead, they developed antibodies that protected them against polio! Salk was thrilled with his success. Carefully he created three separate vaccines, one for each type of polio virus. By the summer of 1952, he felt ready to try his vaccines on humans.

On June 30, Salk drove to the small town of

Leetsdale, Pennsylvania, to visit the D. T. Watson Home for Crippled Children. The 43 children living there had all been paralyzed by polio. Salk met with directors of the home and the parents of the children who lived there.

"I'm asking for your help," he said. "I want permission to inject your children with my new polio vaccine."

"But our children have already had polio!" cried one mother tearfully. "That's why they are paralyzed."

"I understand that," replied Salk gently. "But each child contracted polio from just one virus.

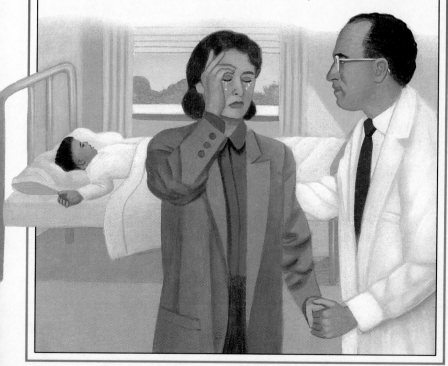

There are two other polio viruses to which they have not been exposed. I would like to give them vaccines for these viruses, and see if they develop antibodies."

"Is it safe?" asked another mother.

"I am convinced that it is safe, based on my experiments with animals," said Salk. "I have run hundreds of tests in my laboratory. But it *is* an experimental vaccine. Your children would be the first humans ever to receive it."

"What happens if something goes wrong?" asked a father.

Salk paused. He didn't want to scare these people. But they had a right to know. As calmly as he could, he explained the risk.

"If the vaccine doesn't work," he told them, "the children could possibly suffer another attack of polio. But my research indicates that the risk is very slim. Please think about it and let me know your decision."

By July 1, he had his answer. The directors and the parents agreed to let him administer the experimental vaccines.

The next day Salk gave each child an injection. In spite of his confidence in the vaccine, Salk did not sleep very well for the next few weeks. He had spent months testing and retesting, but what

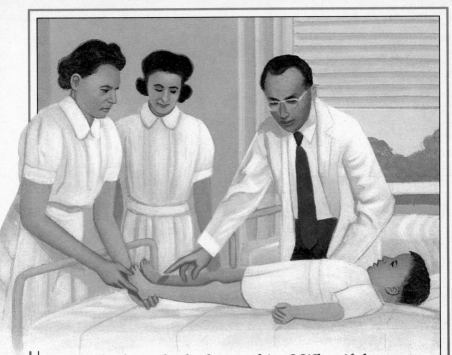

if he had overlooked something? What if the vaccine was ineffective? What if the children developed new cases of polio? All he could do was wait. He visited the Watson Home almost every day to check on the children. After the first month, his hopes rose. None of the children showed any ill effects. And when he tested their blood, he found that they had developed new antibodies!

S ALK'S next step was to try his vaccines on people who had never had any form of polio at all. After long and careful thought, he selected five subjects: himself, his wife, and his three sons.

"But, Jonas," protested a friend, "what if the experiment fails?"

"If I felt there were any chance of failure," said Salk, "I would not administer the test to anyone, family member or not."

Salk spoke these words with deep conviction. He decided to submit his family to the test only because he believed it was completely safe. But again, as with the children at the Watson Home, he would never really know until he had tried it.

Salk discussed the matter with his wife, Donna.

"Someone has to be the first to try it," he said. "If no one ever took a chance, medical science would never progress. Just think of all the people who will suffer from polio in the future if we don't take this risk."

Donna nodded. She knew her husband was right.

"All right," she said. "Let's do it."

Late in the summer of 1952, a nurse came to the Salk home and injected each family member with a polio vaccine. It was a momentous day. Outwardly Salk remained perfectly calm. But inside he felt choked by fear. The next sixty days seemed to pass in slow motion. Every day Salk examined his sons, searching for the slightest sign of illness. No one showed any symptoms of the dreaded disease. Blood tests confirmed what Salk had hoped all along. All five members of the family had developed antibodies!

"We've done it!" cried Salk joyfully. "We've found a way to prevent polio! Thousands of lives will be spared!"

It took another three years to confirm Salk's findings. At last, on April 12, 1955, Dr. Jonas Salk announced the results of his work. He had created a safe polio vaccine.

ACROSS the nation, headlines proclaimed the good news. Because of Salk's work, one of the world's most dreaded diseases would become only a memory.

Overnight, Jonas Salk became a hero. But this dedicated scientist did not care about fame or money. He was content with the knowledge that science had triumphed in the battle against polio.

ROSA PARKS
THE MONTGOMERY BUS BOYCOTT

 When I ride on the city bus, I have to sit in the back. If the bus is full, I must stand up. I have to give up my seat to let a white passenger sit. I pay the same fare that whites do. But the law says that blacks don't have equal rights. That law isn't fair. It just isn't fair.

MRS. Rosa Parks stood on a sidewalk in Montgomery, Alabama. She held a heavy bag of groceries in her arms. As the evening twilight faded into darkness, she sighed softly.

"It's been a long day," she thought. "I'll be glad to get home and put my feet up."

On this day, December 1, 1955, Mrs. Parks had worked all day as a seamstress in a downtown department store. Then she had stopped to do some grocery shopping. Now as she stood at the curb, waiting for the bus, her feet were tired and her arms ached from holding the groceries. Every few seconds she glanced up the street, hoping to see the bus. Finally it pulled up to the curb. The 42-year-old Parks climbed the steps and paid her 10¢ fare.

"Hurry up, move to the back," the bus driver said to her.

Because she was black, Parks could not sit in the front of the bus. That would be against city law. In 1955, there were many laws like that. Blacks could not ride in "white" taxicabs or walk on "white" beaches or attend "white" churches. Parks walked quietly to the rear of the bus and took a seat there.

As the bus made its stops, rush-hour travelers and Christmas shoppers scrambled on board.

Soon there were no empty seats left. At the next stop, two white men boarded the bus. They scanned the seats, looking for a place to sit.

The bus driver also turned around and looked. Seeing that all the seats were occupied, he ordered the blacks to stand up.

"Move back," he shouted to them. "Stand up and make room for these gentlemen."

Parks started to hoist her groceries out of her lap and give up her seat. But then she stopped.

"No," she thought. "No, I'm not going to get up today. I'm just too tired."

Three other black passengers got up and stood in the very back. But Parks did not budge.

"Hey," the driver yelled at her. "Didn't you hear me? I said to move back!"

Parks did not answer. She sat perfectly still, staring out the window at the dark city of Montgomery. The chatter on the bus died down as every passenger turned and looked at her. No one said a word. They all waited to see what would happen next.

"Listen," the driver said, "you get up and stand in the back of the bus, or I'll call the police. You know the law!"

Parks continued looking out the window and pretended not to hear him.

FOR a few moments the driver just sat there, glaring at Parks. He couldn't believe this mild-looking woman wouldn't do what he said. Finally he realized that she was serious. She had no intention of moving. Indignantly, he called to two policemen he saw on the street corner.

Pointing toward Parks, the driver exclaimed, "That woman refuses to give up her seat!"

Parks watched calmly as the policemen approached her. She knew exactly what they were going to do. They were going to arrest her. But she didn't care anymore.

"It's about time someone took a stand," she thought.

"Come with me," one of the police officers demanded. He took Parks by the arm and pulled her to her feet. "You're under arrest."

Parks offered no resistance as the policemen led her off the bus. They took her to the police station, where she was photographed and fingerprinted.

Before taking her to a jail cell, the officer allowed Parks to make one phone call. She called Mr. E. D. Nixon, a leader of the NAACP — the National Association for the Advancement of Colored People.

Parks had been Mr. Nixon's secretary several years earlier. She knew that he could help her. As soon as Nixon hung up the phone, he hurried down to the station. He paid the bail for her release and drove her home. Parks would have to appear in court when her case came to trial.

When she got home, Parks invited Nixon in for coffee. "What will happen next?" she asked him.

"Well," he replied, "it's up to you. You could simply go to court and hope for the best. You could plead guilty, and tell the judge you were just too tired to move. He would probably fine you, and that would be the end of that." Nixon paused. "Or we could make this a test case for all black people. We could attack the law that segregates, or separates, blacks and whites on buses.

We could argue that the law itself is unconstitutional. We could try to put that law on trial."

Parks stirred her coffee. She knew this was a big decision. It could change her life, and the lives of all blacks in Montgomery.

"Let's do it," she said quietly. "Let's challenge that law."

"Think about it carefully," Nixon cautioned her. "Many people will hate you for this, because you are threatening their way of life. You'll probably lose your job. You might even be threatened with violence."

"I know," Parks responded. "I realize it will be unpleasant. But I'm tired of the way things are. I'm willing to take the risk. Maybe something good will come from it."

SO Nixon called a meeting of black leaders. They planned a one-day boycott of the city's buses in support of Rosa Parks and her action. Black people would refuse to use the buses. The boycott would call attention to the unfair laws.

"The boycott will be held on Monday, December 5," Nixon announced. "That is the day Rosa Parks goes to trial."

The leaders also planned a mass meeting for Monday night. A young minister named Dr. Martin Luther King, Jr., would lead the meeting.

By Sunday, December 4, word of the boycott had spread throughout the black community. Over 40,000 leaflets were handed out. Black ministers gave sermons on the importance of the boycott. In black barbershops, stores, and restaurants, people talked about it. The city's eight black taxi-cab companies joined the fight. They agreed to drive boycott participants around the city for the regular bus fare of one dime.

ON Monday morning, Parks woke up early. She tried to stay calm, but her hand shook as she poured her coffee. It still surprised her to think that she was going to appear in court.

"Are you worried?" asked her husband.

"Not really," said Parks. "I know what will happen. The judge will declare me guilty of breaking the law. But then we're going to appeal the decision all the way to the Supreme Court. What I'm really worried about is the boycott. If it doesn't work, people won't pay any attention to this case."

Parks was not the only one who was worried. Black leaders around the city held their breath, waiting to see if the boycott would work. Dr. King got up at 6:00 A.M. and rushed to his front window. He stood there watching for the buses that drove past his house every morning.

"I'll be happy if more than half the regular black riders stay off the buses," King told his wife.

As the first city bus rolled down his street, King cried out in joy. "Look! There's not a single black person on that bus!"

The boycott was almost one hundred percent successful. Blacks hitchhiked to work. They rode horse-drawn carriages. One even rode a mule. Some walked with their arms linked together, singing songs. Others walked alone, their heads held high. That entire morning King saw only eight blacks riding buses.

Meanwhile, Parks walked solemnly into the courthouse. The case did not take much time. Rosa Parks had definitely broken the law. The judge found her guilty and fined her $10 plus $4 court costs. Parks smiled as her lawyer announced plans to appeal the decision.

That night thousands of blacks attended the mass meeting led by Dr. Martin Luther King, Jr. His inspiring words urged them to claim their rights as U.S. citizens.

"We are tired — tired of being segregated and humiliated; tired of being kicked around," said King. "We have no choice but to protest."

The people cheered and clapped wildly. By the end of the meeting, they decided to continue the bus boycott. They wanted to get rid of the law segregating blacks on buses. They knew it might take a long time. But they didn't care. For the first time, they were standing up together and demanding their rights. It felt good. The fight had begun.

Months dragged by, but the boycotters did not give up. The city's 42,000 blacks steadfastly refused to ride the buses. They found other ways to get to their jobs. The bus companies lost thousands of dollars. But the city stubbornly refused to change the law.

INALLY Parks's case reached the United States Supreme Court. On November 13, 1956, the Supreme Court justices declared the law unconstitutional. They said that blacks were entitled to the same rights on buses as whites.

When Parks heard the news, she cried with relief and joy.

"It's been a long, hard fight, but it was worth it!" she exclaimed.

The blacks of Montgomery agreed with her. They felt enormously grateful to Parks. She had been willing to sacrifice her personal well-being to help others. True to Nixon's prediction, she had lost her job. But Parks was content. Something good *had* come from her decision.

Rosa Parks had done more than just refuse to give up her seat. She had taken a stand for progress and justice. Her courageous deed helped unite blacks and sparked the Civil Rights Movement. Rosa Parks had inspired others to stand up and fight for their rights.

BUDDY HOLLY
ROCK 'N' ROLL PIONEER

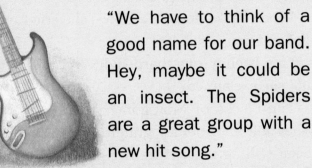

"We have to think of a good name for our band. Hey, maybe it could be an insect. The Spiders are a great group with a new hit song."

"Let's see. What are some insects? How about the Beetles?"

"No, beetles just get stepped on."

"Listen. Do you hear something?"

"Yeah, it's a cricket chirping."

"How about the Crickets?"

"The Crickets. Hmmm. I like the sound of that. Buddy Holly and the Crickets."

CHARLES Hardin Holley loved to make music. When he was just a toddler, he bounced around the house singing tunes his mother had taught him. In 1941, when he was five, his parents entered the young musician in a local talent show. There "Buddy," as he was nicknamed, won five dollars in a singing contest.

"You know," said Mr. Holley at dinner that night, "Buddy has real talent. I bet one day he'll have a career in music."

It seemed silly to talk about careers when their son was only five. Still, Buddy *did* show great promise. When he saw a violin in a store, he ran over and tried to play it. At age eleven he began playing the piano. Eventually, Buddy found his real love: the guitar.

"I don't know why," he told his parents with a grin, "but there's just something about a guitar that I can't resist."

The Holleys did all they could to encourage Buddy's growing interest in music. They made sure their home in Lubbock, Texas, was well stocked with records. They even helped Buddy convert the family garage into a room where he could practice his music. Every week he listened to the Grand Ole Opry broadcast on the radio from Nashville, Tennessee.

In 1951, at the age of fifteen, Buddy came to them with an idea.

"Bob and I want to form a band," he said. Indeed, he and his long-time friend Bob Montgomery had been talking about this idea for months.

Before Mr. or Mrs. Holley could say a word, he presented his reasons. "I know we're young, but we've got a lot of good ideas for songs. We've been working on arrangements for several tunes, sort of a combination of country and western and the new bop. We want to call ourselves 'Buddy and Bob.'"

After pouring out his plan, Buddy took a deep breath and looked at his parents anxiously.

"Well?" he asked. "What do you think?"

The Holleys smiled at their son. Buddy was so enthusiastic about the idea, it would have been hard to say no. Buddy and Bob had already performed at school functions. It seemed a natural step for the boys to seek a wider audience.

"Go right ahead, son," said Mr. Holley with a nod of his head. "Give it a try. We're behind you all the way." The Holleys were proud of Buddy's drive to succeed.

Buddy and Bob played every chance they got. They played at promotional openings for food markets and car dealerships. They became popular in the clubs and dance halls around Lubbock.

"Hey, Buddy," one of his friends teased, "who ever heard of a singing star with glasses? You should get rid of those ugly things!"

Buddy thought about it. Maybe glasses *were* bad for his image. The next night he played without them. Unfortunately, he dropped his guitar pick and had to get down on his hands and knees to find it. From then on Buddy stubbornly resisted advice to get rid of his glasses.

"They just want me to fall right off the stage, that's all," he declared to his mother. "If people are going to like me, they'll just have to like me with my glasses on."

IN October 1955, Buddy and Bob opened shows in Lubbock for Bill Haley and the Comets, Elvis Presley, and Marty Robbins. A Nashville agent saw the shows and was impressed.

"I'd like you boys to prepare a tape for me," he told them. "I'll take it back to Nashville and see if any of the record companies are interested in your sound."

Buddy could hardly contain himself.

"This is it!" he told his parents jubilantly. "This is the big break we've been waiting for."

The two boys prepared the tape, and then waited anxiously to hear from the agent. When the call came, Buddy received it with mixed feelings. Decca Records wanted him, but not his partner. Buddy considered turning down the offer.

"I don't know what to do, Bob. I feel terrible about this," he agonized.

"For as long as I've known you, you've been talking about making a record," Bob replied. "Now you've got your chance — go ahead!"

So, Buddy went to Nashville. He made several records. But neither he nor the people at Decca were pleased with them.

"They told me they wanted a rock 'n' roll singer," Buddy complained to Bob on the phone. "But they don't even know what rock 'n' roll is."

"What do you mean?" Bob asked.

"Well, these guys are big-time producers. But country music is all they know. They're trying to make me into a rockabilly singer, and that's just not what I am. I have a bad feeling about this."

Buddy's intuition was right. None of his records did well, and Decca dropped his contract.

SADDER but wiser, Buddy returned to Lubbock. There he and three friends formed a new group called Buddy Holly and the Crickets. The Crickets were Niki Sullivan, who played lead guitar, Joe Mauldin on bass guitar, and Jerry Allison on drums.

Through the fall and winter of 1956, Buddy and the Crickets practiced in the Holley family garage. Buddy created songs like "That'll Be the Day," and together the group worked out the best way to play them.

"Our music sessions are pretty informal," Buddy told his father. "I guess they have to be since I can't read music!"

When the group had arranged several new songs, Buddy decided to make another try at stardom. He and the Crickets traveled to a recording studio in Clovis, New Mexico. There, with the help of the studio's owner, Norman Petty, they recorded their songs.

"I like your songs," Petty told Buddy. "I like them a lot. If you'll take me on as your manager, I think I can get a record contract for you."

Again Buddy felt his hopes soar. But this time he didn't allow himself to get too excited. "I hope it works out," he told his parents, "but if not, I won't be as crushed as I was the last time."

Buddy didn't need to worry. Petty knew what he was talking about, and he soon landed Buddy and the Crickets not one, but two contracts.

"Brunswick Records will sign the Crickets as a group," he told Buddy. "And their other studio, Coral Records, will sign you as a solo artist."

"Okay," Buddy told Petty, grinning broadly. "It's a deal."

In June 1957, Buddy released his first single record, called "Words of Love." It took off slowly. But his first record with the Crickets, a polished new version of "That'll Be the Day," became an instant hit. His last name appeared on the label spelled without an *e*. He decided not to correct it and use "Holly" from then on.

WITH the release of the two records, Buddy Holly exploded onto the national music scene. His unique musical style swept the country, dazzling teenagers from coast to coast. In 1958 he had a string of hits, including "Peggy Sue," "Rave On," and "Early in the Morning." And with the Crickets, he made such classics as "Oh Boy," "Maybe Baby," and "It's So Easy." Young people everywhere adored the upbeat lyrics, the new rhythms, and the playful feeling of freedom of his songs. Just listening to this new music made them want to join in and dance.

They also loved his trademark "hiccup" sound, which turned a word like "Sue" into "Sue-a-oo."

As soon as the records began taking off, the group received numerous booking offers. They agreed to do a week of shows on the East Coast. At this time, no pictures existed of Buddy Holly and the Crickets. Because of their music, promoters assumed they were black. The Crickets played to all-black audiences in Baltimore, Washington, D.C., and at the Apollo Theater in New York. They were enthusiastically received and enjoyed themselves greatly. They were glad this "mistake" had been made.

A succession of other tours soon followed. To Buddy, it was a dream come true. As their songs climbed the charts overseas, the Crickets booked tours in Australia and England. They were big hits in both countries. They especially made an impression in England. One reviewer proclaimed, "Take my word for it — this is rock 'n' roll like we've never heard it before."

THE Crickets introduced the idea of a tightly knit, guitar-oriented band that wrote its own songs and shared the limelight. Many new English groups patterned themselves after the Crickets' format of drums, bass, and lead and rhythm guitars.

Buddy insisted on controlling the recording of his songs. He was one of the first musicians to double-track his voice and guitar. When Niki, the other guitarist, left the group, Buddy had to play both lead and rhythm. He became a great stylist. He even used strings to back up his music.

Sadly, this skyrocketing career was cut short. Buddy Holly died in a plane crash on February 3, 1959, at the age of 22, while on tour.

But Buddy Holly left his mark on a whole generation of musicians. Groups like the Beatles and Rolling Stones were influenced by his style and recorded some of his songs. This tall, slim boy from West Texas remains one of the giants of rock 'n' roll. His music will never fade away.

ROBERTO CLEMENTE

MORE THAN AN ATHLETE

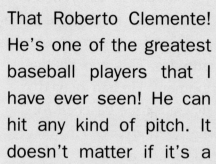

That Roberto Clemente! He's one of the greatest baseball players that I have ever seen! He can hit any kind of pitch. It doesn't matter if it's a fastball, a curve ball, a knuckle ball, a sinker, or a slider. He can hit 'em all. And in right field he's a terror! That powerful throw of his gets the runner out almost every time! What a guy! A great ballplayer and much more besides!

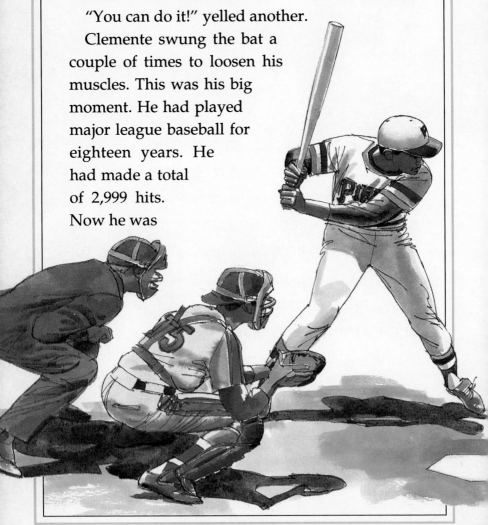

HEN Roberto Clemente stepped into the batter's box on September 30, 1972, the crowd went wild. People cheered and whistled. They waved their hats and stomped their feet.

"Go for it, Roberto!" screamed someone in the stands behind home base.

"You can do it!" yelled another.

Clemente swung the bat a couple of times to loosen his muscles. This was his big moment. He had played major league baseball for eighteen years. He had made a total of 2,999 hits. Now he was trying for number 3,000. Everyone on his team, the Pittsburgh Pirates, was rooting for him. So were all the fans in Three Rivers Stadium and the millions of people who sat watching the game on TV or listening to it on the radio.

"Only ten players have 3,000 hits," Clemente thought to himself. "I sure would like to be the eleventh."

He tightened his grip on the bat. Then, as always, he gave a last-minute jerk of his head to get his back in position. The pitcher hurled a fastball over the plate. Clemente took a giant swing and drilled the ball into left center field for a double.

He had done it! He had really done it! As he stood on second base catching his breath, Roberto Clemente waved and smiled broadly.

"This is one day I'll never forget," he thought proudly.

Clemente had many reasons to be proud. His mind drifted back to his childhood, growing up in Puerto Rico near the sugar cane fields. There, in a rough clearing, he had played baseball with his friends. He remembered the homemade balls they used because they couldn't afford real ones.

"All the boys wanted to be professional baseball players," thought Clemente. "But only a lucky few made it."

Clemente, one of the lucky few, accomplished many great things in the major leagues. He won the batting title four times. In 1966 sportswriters named him the Most Valuable Player in the National League. That same year his fellow players voted him Outstanding Player of the Year. He played in twelve All Star games. And he was awarded the Golden Glove eleven years in a row.

More importantly, perhaps, Clemente had also helped break down the racial barriers in the game of baseball. When he first joined the Pirates, many people resented the presence of Hispanics and blacks in the game. Clemente was the target of many hateful comments because of his race. But he ignored these remarks and concentrated on his playing. Over time he earned the respect of everyone, fans and critics alike.

A FTER the game that day, Clemente felt terrific. The baseball season was ending, and he was already looking forward to next year. Who knew what records he might set in 1973?

"I'm glad for some time off," he told his teammates. "It will give me the chance to work with my other team back home."

Clemente had agreed to manage Puerto Rico's team in the Seventh Annual World Series for Amateur Baseball. Clemente remained very attached to his home in Puerto Rico. He and his wife, Vera, and their three sons lived there during the off-season. All their family and closest friends lived there, too. Clemente had never forgotten his boyhood friends, most of whom worked on sugar cane plantations.

"I want to help as many people as I can," he explained to Vera. "I have been very lucky, and now I want to help others. I would like to build a sports park where children could receive athletic training. They should have a real baseball diamond and decent equipment." Clemente asked the Puerto Rican government for funds to begin his project. But he got no response.

In November 1972, Clemente took his amateur team to Managua, Nicaragua, to compete in the Amateur World Series. During his visit, Clemente was struck by the poverty of many Nicaraguans. It pained him to see young children begging on the streets.

One day he stopped by a hospital in downtown Managua. There he made friends with Julio, a fourteen-year-old orphan, who had lost both legs in an accident. Clemente was touched by the plight of this brave young boy.

"What will happen to Julio?" he asked a nurse.

"I don't know," she replied. "If he had $750, we

could fit him with artificial legs. But, poor thing, he has no money."

Clemente took this as a challenge. He and his team raised the money for Julio's new legs.

RETURNING to Puerto Rico, Clemente celebrated Christmas with his family. According to island traditions, the holiday season stretched from early December to early January. It was a happy time for Clemente, a time for enjoying the company of his family and friends. His family hosted many fiestas. During these parties, the house rang with music and laughter. Many times Clemente sat at the family's big electric organ, playing songs for his guests.

"Yes," he thought as he sat surrounded by loved ones, "I have been lucky. I am very, very fortunate."

Then, on December 23, Clemente heard some upsetting news. An earthquake had hit the city of Managua, Nicaragua. It had killed 6,000 people and injured almost 20,000 more. In addition, it had destroyed thousands of homes.

Clemente remembered the poor conditions he had seen the previous month. He could imagine the plight of the people now.

"I must do something," Clemente cried when he heard the news. "Those people need help."

Clemente thought about what he could do. He decided to organize a relief fund for the people of Managua.

"We can use the stadium in the middle of San Juan," he said to his friend Ruth Fernandez, who also wanted to help. "People can leave their donations of food and clothing there."

As word of the relief effort spread, donations poured in. Puerto Ricans gave not only clothing and food, but medicine, household supplies, and cash. Clemente spent all Christmas Day working in the stadium, organizing the donations.

"Take a break, Roberto," urged Ruth at last. "Go get some rest, and have something to eat."

"No," said Clemente, "not while there is still so much to be done." He continued working late into the night and all the next day.

By December 27 he was ready to go home and get some sleep. But first he arranged to stay in constant touch with the Managua Airport from his home.

"I need to make sure that everything goes smoothly," he told his wife. "Nothing must delay the shipment of these relief materials."

On Friday, December 29, Clemente finally felt he could relax. His call for help had been heard, and the people of Puerto Rico had responded.

They had donated 114,000 pounds of relief material and $150,000 in cash to the devastated city of Managua.

"It's good to know that we've helped these people in such sad times," he confided to his wife.

WITH New Year's Eve only two days away, Clemente hoped to turn his attention back to his family. But he received an urgent message from Managua. The city was in need of more medical supplies.

"They must be desperate or they would not make such a request," Clemente said to Ruth. "We will make one last big push to get what they need. I'll rent a plane and arrange to send down another shipment."

Clemente soon found that few planes were available over New Year's weekend. He finally located a cargo plane he could use.

"Great," he thought. "Now if I can only assemble a crew."

He managed to find a pilot, co-pilot, and flight engineer who were willing to go.

"I will go, too," Clemente decided. "I will take charge of unloading and distributing the supplies in Managua once we arrive."

On the morning of the flight, Ruth took Clemente aside. "Don't go, Roberto," she pleaded. "You're exhausted. You haven't had any sleep in days. Besides, it's New Year's Eve. Stay here with your children and Vera."

Vera, too, asked Clemente to stay. But he looked at both women with the quiet determination they knew so well.

"I really feel that I should go. People are suffering. And I am worried about Julio. I want to see if I can find him."

Clemente hesitated and turned to his wife. "Do you mind terribly?"

Vera smiled at him. "No," she said softly. "I understand. Do what you have to do."

Clemente waited at the airport while the plane underwent minor repairs. It finally took off at a little past 9:00 P.M. But as it rose over the water, something went wrong. Suddenly the plane plummeted through the air, crashing off the coast of Puerto Rico. It came down in turbulent seas a mile and a half from shore. The wreckage was not found until January 2. There were no survivors.

CLEMENTE'S death stunned the people of Puerto Rico and his fans back in the United States. No one could believe that the talented, energetic ballplayer was really dead. The fact that he died while trying to help the Nicaraguans touched people deeply.

After Clemente's death, the government of Puerto Rico and his widow decided to honor him by making his dream a reality. They raised money to build the Roberto Clemente Sports City in his hometown of Carolina, Puerto Rico. Today the sports center stands as a fitting monument to a great athlete and a man who always did whatever he could to help others.

MAX CLELAND
HERO FOR LIFE

Just a few more weeks and I would have been out of Vietnam. Then — in one split second — my whole life changed! Now I'm minus one arm and both legs. Stunned, I turned to the Veterans Administration for help. But they had nothing for me. Nothing. Is this the best America can do?

MAN, you should be happy," a friend told Lieutenant Max Cleland in the spring of 1967. "You've got it made! Right now you could be jumping out of planes in Vietnam. But instead, you've got this nice soft assignment in New Jersey. Some guys have all the luck!"

Cleland knew his friend was right. He *was* lucky to get this assignment. Trained as a paratrooper in the U.S. Signal Corps, he could have been sent to the war zone. Instead, he was an aide to a general at Fort Monmouth.

"If I'm so lucky, then why am I unhappy?" Cleland wondered.

As the weeks wore on, Cleland discovered the answer.

"I feel guilty," he explained to General Thomas Reinzi. "I don't feel right about shaking hands and attending parties while other men with less training are being sent to fight in Vietnam."

General Reinzi gave Cleland a stern look. "Listen, son," he said. "You've earned it. You were an outstanding student in high school and college. You've almost completed your master's degree. I think you deserve this assignment. What makes you so eager to risk your life by going to war?"

"I feel that it's my duty, sir," replied Cleland. "I'd like to request a transfer to Vietnam."

Within weeks Cleland's request was granted. He was sent to Vietnam as part of the First Air Cavalry Division. He soon learned that fighting this war had little to do with glory or honor or freedom. Dropped into the hot, wet jungles of Vietnam, the soldiers struggled just to stay alive. At any moment they knew they might step on hidden mines or walk into an ambush.

Despite the chaos, Cleland managed to keep up his spirits. He made close friends among his fellow soldiers, and always did whatever he could to help them. His intelligence, courage, and positive attitude soon won him the rank of captain.

In early 1968, a series of bloody battles broke out in the Vietnamese village of Khe Sanh. During one fight, Cleland's troops risked their lives to deliver first aid to others on the battlefield. As commander of the unit, Cleland was awarded the Silver Star.

By spring of 1968, he was exhausted. Cleland had only five weeks left of his tour of duty. His thoughts turned to home.

Suddenly, Cleland's fate changed. On April 8, 1968, he flew by helicopter to a hilltop near Khe Sanh. When the chopper lifted off, Cleland looked back and saw a hand grenade lying on the ground, near where the helicopter had been. He

went to pick it up and dispose of it. He didn't know that it was "live."

Just before Cleland reached the grenade, it exploded. The blast blew him backwards. The roar of the explosion deafened him for a moment and blurred his senses. When he blinked open his eyes, he saw that his right hand was gone. He moved his head slightly. His right leg and left foot were gone, too.

Through the haze, he fought to stay conscious. "I must stay awake," he thought desperately. "I must not let myself go to sleep. If I'm awake, then I'm alive. And I've got to stay alive."

Cleland was rushed to a field hospital, where his wounds were bandaged. Nine days later he was moved to a military hospital at Quang Tri for an operation.

WHEN he woke up after the operation, he learned that both legs had been amputated, or cut off, above the knee. And his right arm had been amputated at the forearm.

"How are you feeling?" asked a nurse when she saw that Cleland had awakened.

Cleland tried to answer, but he choked on his words. It didn't matter. He didn't want to talk anyway. He just wanted to curl up and die. Staring in horror at the bandages, he started to cry.

The next day he was flown to Walter Reed Hospital in Washington, D.C. There doctors worked to help him recover.

At first, he felt close to despair. "I don't want to recover," he said bitterly. "I'm never going to have my arm and my legs back. My life is over."

Each day he felt more defeated and depressed. A cloud of darkness settled around him. But then one night, as he lay in his hospital bed, something happened. A strong, primitive urge overtook him. He could almost hear a voice talking to him. "Live on," it said. "Your life is not over yet. Think of what you *can* do, not what you can't do."

FROM that moment on, Cleland began his slow, but determined process toward recovery. He used every ounce of strength to cope with his disabilities. The simplest things were a challenge. With just one hand, he learned how to zip a zipper. Tie a

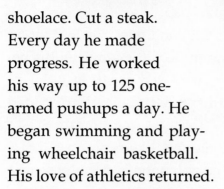

shoelace. Cut a steak. Every day he made progress. He worked his way up to 125 one-armed pushups a day. He began swimming and play-ing wheelchair basketball. His love of athletics returned.

Eventually, Cleland was transferred to a V.A., or Veterans Administration, hospital. Here, Cleland met a new obstacle to his recovery. Staff workers discouraged all his at-tempts to live a normal life.

He asked them to teach him to drive a special car. They refused. He requested his own personal wheelchair. It took a year for it to arrive. He asked for the back pay that the Army owed him. No one offered to help him get it.

The most difficult moment came when he asked to be fitted with artificial legs so he could learn to walk again.

"Forget it," advised one doctor. "You've lost both legs and an arm. You'll never be able to use artificial legs."

"That's not true!" cried Cleland. "Just give me a chance, and I'll prove it to you."

It took Cleland many months of pleading to get the V.A. to give him a pair of artificial legs. And even then he didn't get good ones. He had to use uncomfortable wooden pegs for four months before he finally received jointed plastic legs.

The V.A.'s treatment left Cleland frustrated and angry.

"The V.A. made me feel like a number, not a human. No one cared about me or my problems," he said.

As Cleland made the adjustment to life outside the hospital, he decided to enter politics. He ran for the Georgia state senate, and won. During his

two terms, he sponsored a bill to give veterans more free education. He also fought for laws to require public buildings to have access for the handicapped.

As time passed, Cleland decided to stop using the artificial legs he had fought so hard to get. They were painful and tiring. He realized he could travel faster in a wheelchair. He felt ready to face the world as he really was. He knew his strength did not come from artificial legs. It came from his commitment and drive to succeed.

TIME did not allow Cleland to forget his unpleasant experiences with the Veterans Administration. He wanted to find a way to improve this important federal agency.

"There are eight million Vietnam era veterans in this country," he told himself. "Two million are disabled. The V.A. should be helping these men and women to rebuild their lives — not discouraging them."

In 1975, Cleland joined the staff of the Senate Veterans' Affairs Committee. There he became responsible for checking on the medical care of veterans. He visited many V.A. hospitals to gain firsthand knowledge about the conditions and care of patients. He criticized hospital workers for their lack of hope and optimism for their patients.

He called for the V.A. to show more compassion. And he urged V.A. hospitals to give better counseling to Vietnam vets.

"Vietnam veterans need help readjusting to society," he said. "It's great to conclude peace on the battlefield, but the most important thing for each veteran is to conclude peace within his own mind."

Cleland's outspoken attitude caught the attention of fellow Georgian Jimmy Carter. When Carter became President of the U.S. in 1977, he asked Cleland to head the Veterans Administration.

Cleland was stunned. "The V.A. has a $19 billion budget!" he exclaimed. "It has more than 200,000 employees. It would be a great challenge … but I'm not sure I have the experience."

As Cleland spoke these words, he remembered a famous quote by Aldous Huxley: "Experience is not what happens to a man; it's what a man does with what happens to him."

Cleland realized that in some ways he had plenty of experience to offer the V.A. And he loved the idea of putting his beliefs into action. In February 1977, 34-year-old Max Cleland became the youngest man ever to head the Veterans Administration. He also became the first Vietnam veteran and the first amputee to hold the post.

IN his first months on the job, Cleland sent out clear signals of the changes he planned. No longer would V.A. hospitals be drab, dreary, and full of gloom. Cleland ordered fresh paint for all hospital walls, a symbol of the fresh new spirit he hoped to build. He planned long-term treatment programs for alcoholics, and counseling groups for troubled vets. He computerized the V.A. records to speed requests for equipment. He brought a sense of change and vitality to the musty old halls of the V.A.

As Cleland guided the Veterans Administration through these changes, he knew he stood as a powerful symbol to many Americans. He served as a public reminder of the Vietnam War, and of the pain that many vets had suffered. He was also living proof that people could live full lives with even the most severe physical limitations. To all Americans, he symbolized courage, healing, and hope for the future.

CANDY LIGHTNER
THE BATTLE AGAINST DRUNK DRIVING

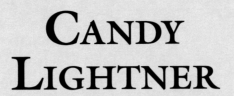

I really do love my mom, but there are times when she makes me so angry! Ever since my twin sister, Cari, was killed by a hit-and-run driver, she won't let me do anything. We have a terrible fight every time I want to go somewhere with my friends. I guess she's afraid that something bad might happen to me, too.

CANDY Lightner pulled her car into the driveway of her California home on May 3, 1980. She was late coming back from shopping and was in a hurry to start supper. As she stepped out of the car, her ex-husband Steve and her father came walking toward her.

"Honey," said Steve slowly, "we've lost Cari."

Candy smiled and patted him on the back. She assumed that her 13-year-old daughter had gone to a friend's house.

"It's okay. We'll find her," she said.

"She's not missing, Candy," Steve replied in a distressed voice. "She was struck by a hit-and-run driver. She's dead."

The words seemed to slap Lightner in the face. She couldn't believe it. "No!" she cried. "You must be wrong! Not Cari!" Then she slumped against the car and fainted.

For the next few days, Lightner lived in a blurry nightmare. She couldn't eat, couldn't sleep. She felt consumed by grief. At the funeral she sat numbly, staring into space. When it was over, she drove to meet several close friends at a restaurant. On the way, she passed the scene of the accident. Lightner saw police officers on the side of the road, measuring skid marks.

"This is it," Lightner whispered to herself.

"This is the site. Cari was right here—walking in the bike lane."

A wave of nausea swept over her. Abruptly she stopped the car and walked over to the officers. She told them who she was.

Choking back her tears, she asked one of them, "Have they caught the driver?"

"Yes, ma'am," replied the officer. "He's at the station right now. His name's Clarence Busch. He was drunk when he killed your daughter."

"Drunk?"

"That's right, ma'am. And this isn't the first time, either. He's been arrested for drunk driving three times in the last four years. In fact, just two days before hitting your daughter, he was arrested for a previous hit-and-run. He was out on bail when he hit your child."

Candy felt her sorrow turning to outrage.

"How much prison time do you think he'll get?" she asked.

"Lady, you'll be lucky if this guy gets any jail time, much less prison."

Candy stared at the officer in disbelief. "What do you mean? Why would the courts turn a killer loose?"

The officer shrugged. "That's just the way the system works," he told her. "Drunk drivers get off light."

"But that's not fair!" she protested.

"Well, that's just how it is," the officer responded.

DAZED, Lightner drove to the restaurant. She told her friends what she had learned.

"I just can't believe it! That man killed Cari because he was driving while he was drunk, and he's not even going to be punished for it. It makes me sick!" The more Lightner thought about it, the angrier she became.

"I'm going to do something about this," she resolved.

"Candy, be reasonable," one of her friends said gently. "You should just try to forget about it and get on with your life."

Candy set her jaw and brushed back her short dark hair. "I can't forget about it. I'm going to do something to change this mess. I'm going to start an organization."

After a moment of silence, another friend said, "That's a good idea. We can call it MADD — Mothers Against Drunk Driving."

The next day, Lightner began her crusade. She quit her job as a real estate agent and spent the next three months doing research. She was shocked to learn that drunk drivers killed 26,000 Americans every year. She became even more committed to the cause.

She studied traffic laws, punishment codes, and even drunk driving laws from other countries. She sat through long court hearings and observed the way judges handled drunk driving cases. She was amazed at the light sentences judges gave offenders who had repeatedly been charged with drunk driving.

Finally, she could hold her temper no longer. Approaching a judge at the end of a trial, she asked, "Why did you only give that man a warning? He's been arrested for drunk driving six times! He should be put in jail before he kills someone!"

"Well, little lady, I sentenced that man according to the law. If you don't like it, then change the law," the judge replied.

"That's exactly what I intend to do," Lightner answered.

At home, a troubled Lightner discussed the matter with a friend.

"I just can't understand why the laws aren't tougher," she said in frustration.

"Well," the friend replied, "many people, even lawmakers, have occasionally driven a car after too many drinks. They don't want to increase the penalty for drunk driving because they might be the next ones arrested for it."

"That's no excuse! Don't they realize what's at stake? Their child could be the next victim! The laws should be tough. Then people would be afraid to drive when they're drunk."

To get the organization moving, Lightner put up $25,000 of her own money. She used her life savings, plus the insurance money from Cari's death. Working out of her house, Lightner created petitions that demanded tougher laws.

She wrote countless letters to lawmakers urging their support. She put up posters, ran advertisements, and carried the petitions door-to-door.

"MADD has two goals," she told her friends and neighbors. "It will provide support to families of drunk driving victims. And it will fight for tougher drunk driving laws."

She made little progress at first.

"No one seems to care!" she said. "But I'm not going to give up."

MADD *had* to succeed, she told herself. It had to. Otherwise Cari's death would be meaningless.

"If I can raise people's awareness of drunk driving, then I can help get the drunks off the road. I can save other families from the heartbreak that my family has been through."

A FTER a few months, Lightner turned to California Governor Jerry Brown to set up a task force on drunk driving.

"I'd like to make an appointment with the governor," she told his secretary. "I have a very important matter to discuss with him."

"I'm sorry," said the secretary. "The governor is too busy to see you."

Lightner went home disappointed, but the next day she returned to the State House. Again the governor would not see her. Lightner continued going to the State House day after day. She talked with legislative aides, assistants — anyone she could find who would listen to her. Many people expressed sympathy for her cause, but no one offered to do anything concrete to help.

"Well, I know one way to get attention for MADD," Lightner decided.

She contacted a local newspaper about her efforts. The newspaper ran a big feature article on Lightner and MADD. Other papers picked up the story. Finally her message was being heard.

A few days later, Governor Brown's secretary contacted Lightner. "The governor would like to see you," the secretary announced.

Lightner held her breath as she walked into the governor's office. Would he really do something?

"Ms. Lightner, I'm going to create the task force you've been calling for," Governor Brown said. "And I'd like you to be a member."

Lightner was elated. After months of work, she was finally starting to get some results. As a member of the task force, she recommended tougher laws against drunk driving. Governor Brown agreed, and on September 30, 1981, he signed several new drunk driving bills into law.

MEANWHILE, MADD gained strength. Many of the people who joined it had lost loved ones to drunk drivers. But Lightner's message touched others as well. By 1982, MADD had chapters in 29 states. By 1985, it had over half a million supporters, with chapters in 48 states.

"Politicians have to listen to us now," Lightner declared. "We're too big and strong to ignore."

With Lightner leading the way, MADD pushed for tougher drunk driving laws across the nation. It also fought for higher drinking ages. "We just don't feel that kids at 18, many of whom are just learning to drive, should be allowed to drink," Lightner declared. By 1984, 23 states had raised the legal drinking age to 21. That same year Congress passed a law cutting aid to any state that did not raise its drinking age to 21.

"Attitudes *are* changing," said Lightner with

satisfaction. "Some states are banning happy hours in bars. And private companies are starting to offer taxi service for employees who drink too much at office parties."

High school students also became involved. They set up SADD — Students Against Drunk Driving.

Candy Lightner never forgot the pain and loss she and her family had suffered. But Lightner took some comfort in MADD's success. Her one-woman crusade against drunk driving had turned into a national movement. She exposed the problem of drunk driving, and she helped change the laws that dealt with it. By doing that, she helped prevent thousands of tragedies on streets and highways. In many ways, Candy Lightner did the hardest thing of all. She took a senseless tragedy and turned it into an opportunity to make America a better, and safer, place.

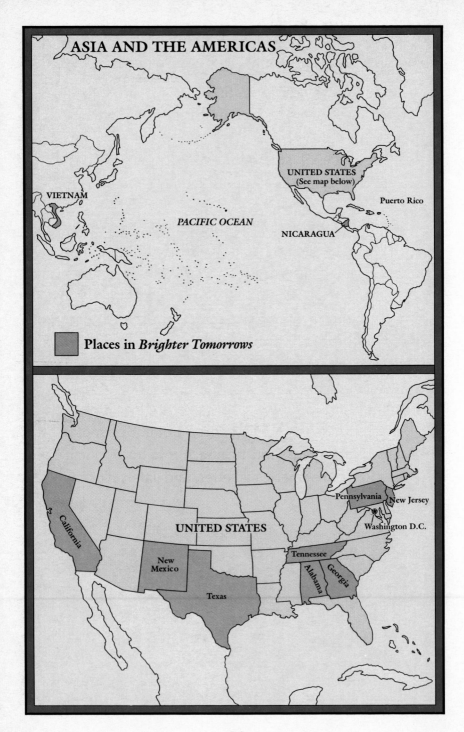

ASIA AND THE AMERICAS

VIETNAM

PACIFIC OCEAN

UNITED STATES
(See map below)

Puerto Rico

NICARAGUA

Places in *Brighter Tomorrows*

California

UNITED STATES

New
Mexico

Texas

Pennsylvania

New Jersey

Washington D.C.

Tennessee

Alabama

Georgia